W9-AWV-633

DISCARD

MERCEDES-BENZ

THE SILVER ARROWS

BY JAY SCHLEIFER

Crestwood House
New York

Maxwell Macmillan Canada
Toronto

Maxwell Macmillan International
New York   Oxford   Singapore   Sydney

629.222
Sch

Copyright © 1994 by Crestwood House, Macmillan Publishing Company

All rights reserved. No part of this book may be reproduced or transmitted in any form or by any means, electronic or mechanical, including photocopying, recording, or by any information storage and retrieval system, without permission in writing from the Publisher.

Crestwood House
Macmillan Publishing Company
866 Third Avenue
New York, NY 10022

Maxwell Macmillan Canada, Inc.
1200 Eglinton Avenue East
Suite 200
Don Mills, Ontario M3C 3N1

Macmillan Publishing Company is part of the Maxwell Communication
Group of Companies.

First Edition
Produced by Twelfth House Productions
Designed by R Studio T

Printed in the United States of America

10 9 8 7 6 5 4 3 2 1

Library of Congress Cataloging-in-Publication Data

Schleifer, Jay.
Mercedes-Benz / by Jay Schleifer.—1st ed.
p.   cm.—(Cool classics)
Includes index.
Summary: Tells the story of the German car company that has been
creating superior, lightning-fast cars for over 100 years.
ISBN 0-89686-815-X
1. Mercedes automobile—History—Juvenile literature.   2. Daimler-Benz
Aktiengesellschaft—History—Juvenile literature.
[1. Mercedes automobile—History.]   I. Title.   II. Series
TL215.M4S27   1994
629.222—dc20   93-17505

CONTENTS

How the jet set get around on the ground...the top-of-the-line SC Class sedan.

 **SHINING STAR**

The time is June 1989. The place is the famous auto race track at Le Mans, France. The event is the 24-hour super race held here each year. You're in the grandstands, and except for the spot behind the wheel of one of the 250-mile-per-hour racers, you've got the best seat in the house. It's right over the start/finish line.

You've been seeing incredible racing action for more than 23 hours now, since the race began at 4:00 P.M. yesterday. You've witnessed wild speed, duels in the darkness, grinding crashes, and frantic pit stops. It's all in the hope of winning Le Mans…the world's longest, most famous race.

You've also seen hopes dashed as Ferraris, Porsches, Nissans, and other racers have limped into the pits like wounded warriors. These cars are tough. But it takes a supreme machine to endure a full day and night of racing.

You smile as the silver Mercedes-Benz C9 streaks past. This car has led the race since it began. Day and night, this machine has turned every turn and straightened every straight like a fine-running clock. It's shown an almost magical ability to get the job done. Some race watchers are beginning to believe that this car can't break down. It's too well made, too perfectly engineered.

But now, with just minutes to go, the Mercedes suddenly slows down and drifts into the pits for an unplanned stop.

*What's wrong? Did the ground-shaking 730-horsepower V-8 engine give up? Has the massive **chassis** cracked under the strain? Or have the huge **disk brakes** finally burned out? Is the Mercedes team having trouble this close to the finish?*

Not quite.

*The car's been called in so that the mechanics can shine up the three-pointed star **emblem** on the hood. That way, the car's* **5** *symbol is sure to stand out in photos taken at the finish.*

A few moments later, the Silver Arrow, as the car is called, crosses the finish line—on time, on schedule, and according to plan.

That's Mercedes-Benz! As the ads used to say, it's "like no other car in the world." Many consider this fine German machine to be the top all-around car in the world. The makers of Mercedes, a company called Mercedes-Benz, actually *invented* the automobile. Gottlieb Daimler and Karl Benz were the first engineers to attach a gasoline motor to a set of wheels.

From those humble beginnings, they built one of the mightiest motor vehicle companies in history! On road or track, Mercedes-Benz has always been among the best of the best.

It's a fascinating story. And you're about to read it.

2 THE AUTOMOBILE'S TWO FATHERS

Gottlieb Daimler swished the yellowish liquid around in a test tube. He stared at it, trying to imagine what secret it held. The stuff was called **benzine** in German and *gasoline* or *petrol* in English.

Scientists had discovered the substance years before. It is made from the black, oily glop called **petroleum,** which comes from the ground. Studies showed that gasoline could be used to clean stains. Gasoline also burns fiercely when its fumes are mixed with air.

The stuff seemed packed with power. Just a few drops produced a big bang when lit. But that was about it. To the earlier scientists, gasoline was simply another interesting chemical with few uses.

But Daimler wasn't about to let the subject go that easily. He was fascinated with gasoline—especially the explosive force it made. It could push the parts of a motor, which could then turn a wheel.

Daimler had been interested in mechanical things for years. Born the son of a baker in 1834, he went to work for a tinsmith when he was young. While working with the tinsmith, he learned about tools and metalworking. Daimler caught on quickly. He was sent to a technical school to perfect his craft. There he learned about inventions of the age, such as the steam engine. After technical school, Daimler worked with different companies building machinery.

Daimler knew that most motors invented at that time were huge, bulky things. They were fine for powering a ship or a train. But they were far too large to move a vehicle transporting only a few passengers. There were some smaller engines, but they lacked power. Nothing could replace the horse for the job of everyday family and cargo transportation.

Karl Benz (left) and Gottlieb Daimler (right).

Yet Daimler also knew that horses were slow and troublesome to keep. The world needed a small, power-packed version of the big engines. Attach a mini-engine to a wheeled vehicle and the world could change! And because gasoline had so much energy, perhaps it could be used to fuel these small engines.

Daimler set a task for himself. He would make a gasoline-powered engine that was small, lightweight, and powerful. The biggest problem would be finding a way to make the gas and air explode at just the right time.

By the mid-1880s, Daimler had done it. He'd created a special tube that glowed red-hot when heated at one end. The gas and air mixture exploded exactly when the switch was turned on.

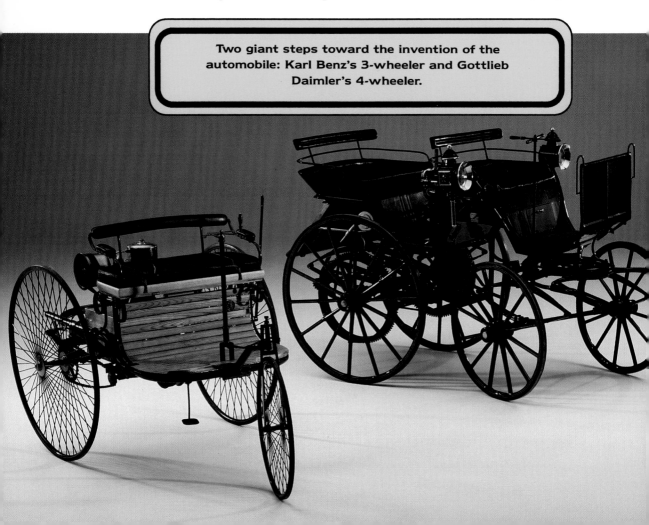

Two giant steps toward the invention of the automobile: Karl Benz's 3-wheeler and Gottlieb Daimler's 4-wheeler.

In 1885, Daimler chose to attach the motor to a two-wheeled contraption that carried one rider on a horselike saddle. He'd made the world's first *motorcycle!* But Daimler knew he'd need a different kind of vehicle to move families and cargo.

Across Germany, Karl Benz had heard of the new lightweight engine. Born in 1844, Karl was the son of a railroad engineer who died when Karl was just two. Benz also studied at a technical college. Now he owned a machine shop. He began to lay out a completely new kind of vehicle that would use the lightweight gasoline engine. He made great progress toward the right combination of engine and machine. But there was still one important difference between his vehicle and the car we know today. The Benz **horseless carriage** had just three wheels. Still, he received a patent for the first practical motor car on January 29, 1886.

Bit by bit, or wheel by wheel, the car was being invented.

The next step in the invention was Daimler's. In 1886, he installed his engine in the first *four-wheeled* horseless carriage. It had room for four people, and the new engine was in the rear. It turned the rear wheels with a thick rubber belt. The right engine and the right kind of vehicle had finally come together. Through the work of both its fathers—two men who never met—the car was born!

 **THE FIRST MERCEDES**

Once the basic design of the automobile had been worked out, the new machine began to sell. But the sales didn't happen on their own.

Daimler and Benz both displayed their new machines at trade shows and fairs. At first there were more doubters than believers. Everyone was interested in seeing the new machine. But nobody wanted to risk money on it.

Finally, after many months, Benz found a customer. The engineer proudly readied the first car to actually be sold. But the customer never took delivery. Before he had a chance, his family had placed him in a mental hospital. Though the man's illness had nothing to do with the car, newspapers used the story to make fun of the new invention.

To improve the auto's image, the two inventors tried advertising. Daimler's ads proudly stated that "horses don't shy away from a Daimler motor."

Then, one day in 1888, Mrs. Benz helped to get sales started. She had to make a 60-mile trip to another town. Ignoring her husband's orders not to touch the car, she cranked it up at 5:00 A.M. while Karl was still asleep. Then she loaded her two children on board and hit the road. When Bertha Benz returned safe and sound, she was both the first female driver and the first person to make a road trip by automobile. People soon began to realize that the car was safe and useful.

In time, the invention began to catch on. Hundreds of horseless carriages began putt-putting around the great cities of Europe and the United States. At first they were driven mostly by wealthy people. But soon the average citizen had joined the horseless age.

As two of the most experienced automakers, both Daimler's and Benz's companies began to grow. Gottlieb Daimler saw only the beginnings of it all. He became ill and died in March 1900, at age 66. Before he died, however, a fleet of Daimler-powered vehicles of all sizes paraded before the old man as he sat on a porch.

Gottlieb's son, Paul, continued his father's dream. And in the early 1900s he made a business deal with a man named Emil

Jellinek. Jellinek would sell Daimler cars in Nice, on the French Riviera.

There was one problem. Germany and France had fought in a war in the 1870s. Jellinek knew that a German-sounding name would be bad for sales. So he asked Paul for permission to rename the cars sold in France after his young daughter, *Mercedes.* Daimler agreed. Soon after, the Daimler Company adopted the Mercedes name for all its cars.

In those same years, the company adopted a new emblem: the famous three-pointed star. Legend has it that Gottlieb had drawn a star on a postcard showing his house back in 1880 and said, "A star shall rise from here, and I hope it will bring blessings to us and our children." Proudly placed on every vehicle built by the company since 1909, it certainly has brought good fortune to the firm!

 **MERGER OF GIANTS**

Both the Daimler and Benz companies continued to grow through the start of World War I. When the war began, in 1914, the companies were asked to build equipment for war at their large factories, located in several German cities. The equipment included aircraft engines.

Some of the finest engines of the war came from the Daimler and Benz plants. But they were built for a losing cause. Germany was defeated in 1918.

Because almost all the fighting had been done outside of Germany, the two companies' factories were undamaged. But the victorious nations made the German people pay huge amounts of money as punishment for starting the war. The German people

The 1902 model was among the first to carry the Mercedes name.

When the Daimler and Benz companies merged in the 1920s, their biggest sellers were four-door sedans like this 1928 model.

had no money left to buy new cars. All automakers, including Daimler and Benz, suffered a drop in sales. Several companies, in fact, went out of business.

To survive, the two weakened giants agreed to merge in 1926. From then on, the combined company would be called Daimler-Benz. Its cars would carry the name Mercedes-Benz.

The new firm had a wide range of models, large and small. But as if to celebrate the merger, they now produced one of the most outstanding cars of all time: the Mercedes-Benz Model Type K series.

The K was developed from an earlier series of larger, less powerful cars. To create the K, which first stood for *kurz* (short), engineers lightened the previous chassis. Then they added a **supercharger** to the car's 6-cylinder engine for even more power. The new lighter, stronger machine had a full 160 horsepower.

This was major muscle for the time. To make room for the large engine's exhaust, out on the streets, the designers cut three huge slots in the side of the hood. Through these, they ran thick, insulated exhaust pipes.

With this raw power, the K was not for timid drivers. But experienced sports car fans loved it! They helped the new car become known as one of the real road burners of the 1920s.

But the K was only the beginning. It was followed by the S, or Sports model. This machine was lighter and faster than the K. There were also the SS, or Super Sports, which was even faster than the Sports model, and the SSK, with superchargers. Finally, there was the SSKL, in which the final L stood for *leicht* (lightweight).

Through this alphabet game, Mercedes-Benz lightened the original car several times. And it boosted the auto's power several times more. The result was pure driving excitement—and one of the world's great automobiles. The SSK model is so classic that kit car makers still build fiberglass copies of it for those who were born too late to enjoy the original!

Mercedes also used the late 1920s to develop an incredible sedan: the Type 770, also known as the Grosser, or grand Mercedes. True to its name, this monster featured a 7.7-liter, 8-cylinder engine complete with a supercharger. Designed to be **chauffeur**-driven, the car was meant for royalty. In fact, Grosser models were delivered to Emperor Hirohito of Japan and the ex-king of Germany.

Grosser models were also the favorites of German dictator Adolf Hitler and other high-ranking Nazis. You've probably noticed the evil-looking black cars the Nazis drive in World War II movies. They usually have flags flying off the fenders and scowling storm troopers hanging off the **running boards.** These cars are often Grosser Mercedes, or movie props made to look like them.

No need to learn German to understand the sleek
lines and open exhausts of the 1936 K roadster!

THE SILVER ARROWS TAKE FLIGHT

The Nazis took part in other key events in Mercedes-Benz history—a fantastic string of racing successes of the mid-1930s to late-1930s.

When the decade began, Germany was hit hard by the worldwide economic troubles of those years. One way Germany handled the crisis was to elect a new leader. Adolf Hitler was one of the most evil men in history.

Hitler believed that the Germans were a master race, better than any other people on the planet. Before his 12-year reign was over, he had brought about world war and endless suffering.

While Hitler was in power, he worked to prove that his theory was correct. Sports, including motor racing, was one way to do this. In Hitler's eyes, every German win showed his nation's power over all others.

To ensure victories, the German government pumped huge sums of money into the racing teams of the top German automakers. These companies included Mercedes-Benz and Auto Union.

Mercedes-Benz had always been in racing and had always been successful. But nothing the company had ever done before was quite like the 1930s. When the decade began, the great racing cars were Italy's Alfa-Romeo, France's Bugatti, and a few others. When it ended, the swift silver cars of the Germans were racing against each other. No other cars stood a chance!

The Mercedes-Benz triumph began with a racecar called the W25, which first competed in 1934. This car featured a 400-horsepower, **double overhead camshaft** engine. Its body shell was made of a special lightweight metal. This design was based on aircraft technology.

The W25 was entered in six major races. It won four of them in its first year on the track, a time when most cars are still ironing out the bugs. The other two races were won by Auto Union. A clean sweep by one country was unheard of!

Until 1935, that is. In that year the W25 came back with even more power and was entered in ten major races. It won nine! The following year was Auto Union's, but Mercedes came back even stronger in 1937, with a car called the W125.

If you'd like to put a scare into racing drivers even today, mention the W125. The car's supercharged 5.66-liter straight-8 engine was the Terminator of **open-wheel racing**. It produced a staggering 648 horsepower! Though Auto Union improved its car, the A U never stood a chance against this beast. The big-engined Benz took 7 of the 12 races it entered, leaving the other 5 for Auto Union. The other teams might just as well have stayed home.

"The W125s were thunderous, awesome monsters," wrote one auto expert. "They made strong men grow weak at the knees."

The success didn't end with 1937. In the following two years Mercedes returned with the W154, with its powerful 12-cylinder engine, and the similar W163. These cars won 9 out of 16 top races, while Auto Union took 3 others.

In the final score from 1934 to 1939, Mercedes won *34 of the 48 races it entered.* Auto Union won all but 2 of the others. Since then, no car company has beat that record. And there will probably never be a record like it again.

Great cars were only one reason for this amazing sweep. A great team was another reason. The Germans ran their racing team like an army going into battle. Every straight and turn of a racetrack was studied months before the race. Then the cars were precisely set up for the best performance on each track.

The team would arrive in eight large **diesel** trucks, with as **19**

The awesome W125 racer produced almost as much power as a modern car...in 1937!

many as six cars and 25 mechanics. They'd bring a set of spare engines as well as a bin full of replacement parts. If an unexpected break occurred, one truck zoomed back to the factory to get a new part. The truck was so fast that it might have done well on the track itself!

One story from those years tells how these incredible German racers got their trademark silver color. Until the 1930s the official German racing color was white. In 1934, Mercedes racecars were painted that color. But when they were weighed, they were 2 pounds over the limit. No problem. The mechanics got out the sandpaper and rubbed off every ounce of paint, leaving bare metal. Then they sprayed each car with a light coat of silver paint. The Silver Arrows of Mercedes-Benz got their nickname on that day.

In 1939, auto racing rule makers attempted to break the German winning streak. They made a sudden change in engine-size limits and didn't tell the Germans until the last minute. By the time they told the Germans, the French and Italians already had their new cars fully tested.

Mercedes-Benz had only eight months to create a new car! The company's engineers and mechanics worked night and day to build it. This new car, the W165, ran in only one race before World War II brought an end to the era. But it won!

6 GULLWING!

When Germany invaded Poland in September 1939 and thus started World War II, Daimler-Benz again joined the war effort. The sleek silver racing cars were locked away. And the company's factories switched over to building airplane engines, trucks, and other military vehicles for the German fighting forces.

Daimler-Benz power plants put the muscle in the famed Messerschmitt Bf-109 fighter and the Heinkel He-177 bomber. Both used a supercharged, water-cooled DB-600 series V-12 engine. The engine was mounted *upside down* to allow a sleeker aircraft shape. American and English experts who studied these planes were amazed at the craftsmanship and power of the German engines. This was true even late in the war, when they were built in underground caves, sometimes by slave labor.

By 1945, Hitler's mad gamble to rule the world was over. The dictator had killed himself, and Germany lay in ruins. Always a target for U.S. and British bombers, the giant Daimler-Benz factories had been turned into little more than piles of rubble. "The company," said one saddened D-B manager, "has just about ceased to exist."

Then one of the great business miracles of all times began. Germans started to rebuild their industry. For a year thousands of workers at Daimler-Benz did little more than clean up. Then a handful of vehicles were produced—just over 200 in 1947—from a factory that had once built thousands of cars. But by the early 1950s, output was up to 50,000 a year, with several new models in production. All signs pointed toward future success for the company.

Mercedes officials decided it was time to celebrate. It was time to make some headlines in the car magazines and sports pages and let the auto world know that Mercedes-Benz was back. And there was no better way to do that than to build a hot new sports car. The firm would return to racing!

The new sports car was loosely based on the 300 series sedan model, which was named for its 3-liter, 6-cylinder engine. Designers first placed that engine in a modern, lightweight chassis. The chassis was equipped with **independent rear suspension (IRS).** Then, for a lower hood, they leaned the engine over on its side, as they'd done with the World War II aircraft motors.

To some models they added **fuel injection.** This system sprays fuel directly into the cylinders instead of having it pass through a carburetor. Fuel injection was often used in airplanes. But this was one of the first times it was used in a car.

Around this engine-chassis combination, Mercedes created a slick-looking, lightweight **coupe** body. It still looks sleek and modern, nearly 40 years later.

The body was amazingly strong. Its strength came from wide beams that ran from front to rear under the door openings. The beams were so wide that the usual outward-opening doors wouldn't fit. So Mercedes designers again drew on their aircraft experience. They created doors that swung upward, like a canopy on a fighter plane, or the wings of a sea gull. The world famous Mercedes-Benz 300SL, or Super-Light, gullwing coupe was born!

There's never been a car like the gullwing. Capable of a safe 150 mph, it was the star from the start. Like the Mercedes racers of

The 300SL shows off its "gullwing" doors. The Mercedes-Benz factory still gets letters asking that this model be built again.

the 1930s, nothing could touch it—not the Jaguars, or even most Ferraris. And America's Corvette wasn't even in the same league.

The car was never built in large numbers. Only 1,400 gullwings were made before the design was switched to a roadster with regular doors. But every one is a classic. If you can get a gullwing owner to part with his or her pride and joy, figure on paying about $250,000 to ease the pain!

Two champions: the W196 and Juan Manuel Fangio.

The 300SL's unique doors have since been copied by other automakers. In the 1970s a sports car called the Bricklin featured electric upward-opening doors. Of course, if a fuse blew out, the driver could be trapped inside! Fans of *Back to the Future* movies have seen the gullwing doors of the DeLorean sports car of the early 1980s. Mercedes even used the design on a few experimental cars. But the original remains a true "can't touch this" land-

SAINT MARY'S SCHOOL
309 E. Chestnut Street
Lancaster, Ohio 43130

mark...not just because of unusual doors but because of the great car they were attached to.

⑦ RETURN TO RACING

When Mercedes-Benz announced a return to the track in 1951, the news hit the racing world like an earthquake. Few fans had forgotten how the Silver Arrows had rolled over opponents during the 1930s. And everyone knew that many of the same designers and race managers still worked for the German automaker.

True, there'd be no government money this time, no "master race" ideas to prove. But Daimler-Benz was, and is, one of the world's top car companies. Even without government support, its power towered over small specialists like Ferrari or Porsche. There was a lot to fear.

The return to racing began in 1952. Mercedes brought a special version of the 300SL gullwing coupe to major road races in Europe and North America. Mercedes had prepared for these races with the same thoroughness of the old days. In addition, the company had hired two of the world's top drivers. Juan Manuel Fangio and Stirling Moss worked under the sign of the three-pointed star.

The gullwing specials dominated the 1952 season. Mercedes won various races, including a first and second place at Le Mans. But that was just the beginning. The heavy action came with the W196 racer. This machine dropped like a bomb onto **Grand Prix** racing in 1954.

Grand Prix is the World Series or Super Bowl of motor sports. The cars look much like Indy 500 machines and are just as fast. But they must be nimble enough to race on curvy road courses, not just high-speed oval tracks. Grand Prix cars have always featured the latest in racing technology.

The W196 featured an aircraft-type frame. It was wrapped around a 2.5-liter, 8-cylinder engine that lay on its side in the chassis. The car's 5-speed gearbox was located at the rear. This balanced the front-mounted engine's weight.

The most amazing thing about the engine was its valve system. In most engines, valves, which let gas and air in and draw exhaust gas out, are opened by mechanical pushers and closed by springs. But the W196 engine included mechanical parts that opened *and* closed the valves.

With most cars there was a split second wait before springs slammed and valves closed. But these pushers shut them immediately! As a result, the engine could get on to its next power stroke faster and more precisely.

This system is called **desmodromic** (dez-moh-DROH-mik) **valve gear.** It allowed the W196 engine to spin up to 8,500 revs per minute! No competing engine with valve springs could turn that fast safely or make that much power.

If that were not enough, the car carried a streamlined **aerodynamic** body that covered the wheels for longer races. (There was an open-wheel racing body for the short tracks, where airflow was less important.) And behind the powerful new racer was Mercedes money, preparation, and top driving talent.

Other Grand Prix teams had good reason to be nervous. Mercedes rolled to 11 major wins out of 14 tries, powering Juan Fangio to two World Driving Championships in a row. Winning got so routine that Mercedes officials would decide beforehand which driver should win each race. Fangio was usually told to finish first so he could add to his championship points. But the team manager allowed Moss to win in front of his hometown crowd in England. It was the 1930s all over again!

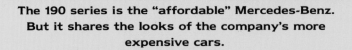

The 190 series is the "affordable" Mercedes-Benz. But it shares the looks of the company's more expensive cars.

Soon Mercedes moved on to the next part of its battle plan: a special two-seat version of the W196 for tracks like Le Mans.

This car, the 300SLR, was driven by Moss and Fangio in the 1955 season. To the W196's fantastic engine and chassis it added the world's first racing **air brake** system. When drivers wanted to slow down, they hit a pedal that threw open a giant metal flap just behind the seats. Racing fans are sure to remember watching the flaps rising and falling as the 300SLRs circled each course.

Stirling Moss reported that the system worked well. But he also noticed something strange. When the air brake was opened, the rear wheels seemed glued to the track. Without realizing it, Mercedes-Benz had discovered **ground effects,** the system of wings and tunnels that's used on today's racers. It forces the wheels downward and makes them stick to the track. But Mercedes was doing so well with what it already had that this was one idea the company didn't build into the car.

Then tragedy hit.

In the 1955 Le Mans race, a slower car suddenly swerved in front of one of the 300SLRs. Mercedes driver Pierre Levegh tried to steer around the car but couldn't. His car slammed into the slower machine. Flung skyward by the collision, the Mercedes sailed into the crowd. Beneath a plume of black smoke, Levegh and more than 80 racing fans were killed.

Although a 300SLR was in the lead, Mercedes ordered its team to drop out of the race in respect for the victims. A Jaguar went on to win. At the end of the season, Mercedes announced it would not race again.

"I don't know when we shall come back," Mercedes-Benz team manager Alfred Neubauer told reporters. "But if we do, there is one thing you can be sure of. There will be no halfway measures. We shall not race again until we have cars that can, and *will,* win."

8 A HOUSEHOLD NAME

For the next 30 years, Mercedes served as one of Europe's most important makers of cars and trucks. Though most Americans know Mercedes for its luxury automobiles, the company also builds a full line of mid-priced models. Mercedes is the German version of Mercury or Oldsmobile. And it always amazes American owners on their first trip to Europe to see "luxury" Mercedes-Benz cars used as taxicabs and police cars.

Not that there aren't Mercedes-Benz luxury cars. Leaders of nations that lack auto industries usually depend on Mercedes for their limousines. A special Grosser model was even built for the pope. Chauffeur-driven, the car had its regular back seat replaced by an electric throne. It could be raised at the touch of a button so that the pope could be seen by the crowds who gathered to watch him pass.

Although the company was not actively racing, sports models were not ignored. The 300SL was the first of a series of modern sportsters that continue to this day. The company's luxurious 500SL two-seater and similar models have been featured on TV shows such as *Dallas* and *Lifestyles of the Rich and Famous.* There's also a mini-sized SL powered by a lawn mower motor. It's sold by the exclusive toy store F. A. O. Schwarz—for several thousand dollars!

Mercedes has become a household name around the world. But people are often confused about how the company names its cars. Actually, it's quite simple. You just have to learn the code.

Most models have a three-digit number followed by letters, such as the 300S, 190D, or 300TD. The number tells you the engine size. A 190 is a 1.9-liter engine. A 300 is a 3.0-liter. And a 500 is a 5.0-liter.

The C in the name of this 500SEC stands for *coupe*.
But it could also stand for *costly, cool,* or *classy!*

The letters usually stand for the model type. "S" stands for a sport model, which is usually a sedan with extra power and better handling. A "T" is a touring model, which Americans call a station wagon. A "C" is a two-door coupe. And an "SL," or sport luxury, is an out-and-out sports car, usually with two seats.

Other letters tell you about the engine. "D" stands for a diesel engine. "E" stands for *Einspritzung*, which is German for fuel injection.

Sometimes the letter "L" is added to an "SE" model. An "L" indicates that the car has a long wheel base.

So, to put it all together: A 300S is a 3.0-liter sports sedan. A 170D is a 1.7-liter diesel. A 300CE is a 3.0-liter fuel-injected coupe. And a 450SL is a 4.5-liter sports car. How about a 500SEL? Well, that's a big 5.0-liter, fuel-injected high-performance sedan with a long wheel base.

Knowing the code makes it easy to figure out what cars' names mean. But it's not so easy to determine the year a Mercedes was built. This is because the cars' looks don't change much, especially around the grille. And that's exactly how the factory wants it. Since the car doesn't look outdated, its **resale value** stays high. Buyers can sell their old cars at a good price and buy new ones often.

What's more, the Mercedes has a look that says "money!" That's why many other carmakers have copied the famous grille. During the 1970s, Ford's Granada, Chevy's Malibu, and Plymouth's Reliant-K all had Mercedes-like grilles. Dodge even built a model called the 600S. The model name was spelled out on the rear in the same kind of chrome lettering the Germans use.

The final copy was on the hood. Where Mercedes puts its famous three-pointed star, Chrysler cars placed a five-pointed star! Chrysler wasn't imitating Mercedes when it chose the star as its emblem in the 1960s. But combined with that grille, the look was very familiar.

But no matter how much the copycats look like a Mercedes, they don't drive like one. The German cars are built with the best materials. They last for years and are capable of extremely high performance.

No wonder! Some German superhighways, called **autobahns**, have *no* speed limits. Drivers can go as fast as they like—and many Mercedes drivers like to go very fast! It's not unusual to see a big Mercedes tearing along in the left lane at 130 mph, while little Volkswagens and Opels jump out of the way. For this kind of driving, a car has to be built right!

It should be noted, though, that the German driver's license test is among the hardest to pass in the world. High-performance cars demand high-performance drivers!

 9 **ON TARGET AGAIN!**

As the 1980s began, big changes hit the luxury car business. There was suddenly strong competition from another German maker, BMW. Then Jaguar of England, which had been having money troubles for years, got its act together and began to compete. Even more competition came from the Japanese.

Until that time, Toyota, Honda, and Nissan had specialized in small, gas-saving cars. Now they began to build luxury models under the names Lexus, Acura, and Infiniti. Some experts said that these new cars were as well made as a Mercedes. But they cost far less.

These new machines challenged Mercedes-Benz. And while Mercedes sat on the sidelines, Jaguar, BMW, and the Japanese

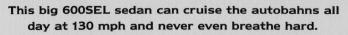
This big 600SEL sedan can cruise the autobahns all day at 130 mph and never even breathe hard.

were out on the racetrack almost every weekend. Could Mercedes bear to stay on the sidelines?

Suddenly, in the early 1980s, the three-pointed star began to appear again in racing. But officially, it wasn't Mercedes that put the emblem there.

A wealthy Swiss racecar designer named Peter Sauber had been building his own race specials for years. At first, he used BMW engines. Then Sauber began working with Mercedes-built power plants.

These Sauber cars with Mercedes-Benz engines were entered in the World Sports Car Championship series. This was a set of races in which Porsche was king and Jaguar and Nissan were strong competitors.

Sauber admitted that the Mercedes factory had given him help. But he insisted that he was the main force behind his effort. Auto experts widely believed that Mercedes was returning to racing through the back door. If the cars won, they would show Mercedes power and skill. If they lost, well, then that would be Sauber's fault.

In fact, Mercedes was doing exactly what Jaguar and others had done to get back into racing. They'd begun working with outside car builders. This made a lot of sense. The factory did not have to hire its own racing specialists. But it could try out new ideas on the track. Meanwhile, the outside builders got help they could never have afforded on their own.

The Sauber-Mercedes cars were design marvels. They were strong and light. Their powerful twin-**turbocharged** 5-liter V-8s started out as versions of the Mercedes sedan engine. But they'd been pumped to produce close to 700 horsepower!

The cars featured **monocoque** (MON-uh-coke) **construction.** This kind of construction replaces the frame and body with a single unit. The suspension systems included ground effects, which Mercedes had discovered in 1955. Ground effects use airflow to

The Sauber-Mercedes cars brought the three-pointed star back to big-time racing.

create a vacuum under the car. This forces the wheels down onto the road for better handling.

The body shapes were tested in the Mercedes-Benz **wind tunnel** for best airflow. And, of course, the cars were finished in silver. A new breed of near 250-mph Silver Arrows had been born.

Sauber-Mercedes cars won major events in 1986 and 1987. And by 1988 Mercedes-Benz was willing to say openly that it had returned to racing.

The 1988 season was all that Mercedes fans had hoped for. There were eight wins, including victories at two of Europe's top tracks: Nurburgring in Germany and Spa in Belgium. But Le Mans and the final series championship were won by Jaguar.

In 1989 Sauber-Mercedes was determined to take home all the trophies. The new C9 racers had the winning edge from day one. And when the checkered flag fell at Le Mans in June, a Silver Arrow was the first to cross the finish line. A few months later Mercedes-Benz had won the world championship for the first time since 1955. The Silver Arrows were scoring bull's-eyes again!

When the 1990 season began, the team's name had changed. "Sauber" was no longer part of it. The Swiss car builder was still involved in producing the cars and managing the racing team. But now the cars were officially Mercedes-Benz Silver Arrows.

Though Mazda won Le Mans in 1990, Mercedes again took the world championship. It was beginning to look like the 1930s and 1950s all over again!

Top Mercedes driver Jochen Mass had something to say about that. "Everyone thinks it has been easy, but that simply isn't true," said Mass. "The only reason we have done so well is that these people in the Sauber team work so hard. They work and work until they get it right."

The chairman of the board of Daimler-Benz backed him up.

"Our long and great tradition in motor sport might make it seem that we think, 'We come, we see, we win!' But the truth is very different. We have had to work very hard for this success."

In 1991, race watchers found out how hard winning was...even for Mercedes. The team returned with a new car, the C291. Because of a change in the rules, the winning twin turbo V-8 engine had been replaced by a flat 12-cylinder design.

Even for the wizards of Mercedes, maybe it was too much to ask that this complicated power plant work perfectly its first season. The car broke down time after time. It was able to finish only one race in the first half of the season. And it won only the last race of the second half.

As for the series championship, Jaguar won the title. The French carmaker Peugeot was second. Mercedes finished third.

At that point, several top teams, including Mercedes and Jaguar, announced they were dropping out of World Sports Car Championship racing. The series had become too expensive and complicated, the teams said. In the end, the company found that it no longer had the power to dominate a racing series as it had in the past. Mercedes added that it would continue to race modified versions of its sedans in a kind of German stock car racing. But this latest return to big-time sports car racing was over.

 # THE FUTURE OF MERCEDES-BENZ

It's been nearly 110 years since Gottlieb Daimler and Karl Benz put the first cars on the road. What does the future hold for the now-giant company they founded?

Like most carmakers, Mercedes does not share its secrets easily.

The latest Mercedes-Benz designs are more rounded and streamlined. This is a 300CE.

But experimental models hint that the company will move strongly down the road of high-tech engineering.

Some of these experimentals have been powered by super-high-performance diesel engines and others have been powered by **hydrogen fuel.** The engineers have tried **rotary engines,** in which a spinning triangle-shaped piston replaces the usual type that moves up and down. Bodies have been built of **composite** materials, which are lighter and stronger than metal. And more and more computers and electronics are being used, even on the standard factory cars.

Safety has always been important to Mercedes. Its cars were among the first in the world to feature air bags. And the car bodies are designed to crumple in a crash. This absorbs the force of the hit and prevents the people inside from being injured. Some SL sports cars even have a metal bar that pops up automatically in a rollover. This helps to keep passengers' heads from hitting the ground. Obviously, advanced safety thinking will play a part in the future of Mercedes.

But no matter what lies under their skins, Mercedes-Benz street models will probably always look somewhat as they do today. The company has learned that maintaining the car's design encourages customer loyalty. Most design improvements will make the air flow more smoothly and easily around those bodies. This usually means a more rounded shape.

What about racing? That's always a question mark with Mercedes. But as the team manager said back in 1955, there will be no halfway measures. When the Silver Arrows show up, they come to win.

You can also count on one more thing. The car's three-pointed star emblem will always shine proudly out front. It's the sign of the world's *first,* and still one of the world's *best,* Cool Classics!

Much has changed between the 1886 and the 1986 models. But the quest for quality and great engineering has stayed the same!

GLOSSARY/INDEX

aerodynamics 27   The study of how air flows over a vehicle; streamlining.

air brake 30   A large movable panel that opens into the airflow, making it harder for air to flow over the body and slowing the car down.

autobahn 35, 36   A German superhighway that often has no speed limit.

benzine 6   The German word for gasoline.

chassis 5, 14, 22, 27, 30   The frame and major mechanical parts of a car attached to the frame. It includes the engine, transmission, and suspension.

chauffeur 15, 31   A worker who drives a car for its owner.

composite 44   A mix of materials that is both strong and light.

coupe 22, 26, 34   A two-door, four-seat sedan.

desmodromic valve gear 27   A system of opening and closing engine valves mechanically instead of with a spring. The design allows for much faster engine speeds and more power.

diesel 19, 34, 44   An engine that burns a heavy fuel oil at high pressure and without needing a spark. Diesels are slow performers but are extremely rugged and low in cost to run. They are often used for truck and tractor engines.

disk brakes 5   A stopping system that works by pressing on a spinning disk attached to a wheel. Disk brakes are especially good in wet weather.

double overhead camshaft 18   A system for quickly opening and closing engine valves. It allows an engine to "breathe better" and make more power.

emblem 5, 11, 35, 44 The visual symbol of a car company, usually shown in a badge on the car. The Mercedes-Benz emblem is the three-pointed star.

fuel injection 22, 34 A system of spraying gas-air mixture directly into the cylinders of an engine instead of having the mixture drift in through a carburetor.

Grand Prix 26, 27 A series of international, open-wheel formula car races.

ground effects 30, 38 The shaping of the underside of a car body to cause a vacuum. The vacuum "sticks" the car to the ground for better handling in turns and at high speeds. The system is used in many racing designs.

horseless carriage 9, 10 A popular early term for automobile.

hydrogen fuel 44 A clean-burning, energy-rich natural gas produced chemically from other substances or by running electricity through water. Some experts think of hydrogen as a fuel of the future.

independent rear suspension (IRS) 22 A means of mounting rear wheels separately to a car chassis so that when one wheel hits a bump and moves, the other is not affected. The system usually provides better handling.

monocoque construction 38 The use of a car body to act as the frame. Eliminating a separate frame cuts weight. Most airplanes use this system. The design is also known as unit construction.

open-wheel racing 19, 27 Racing in which the car's wheels are located outside the body.

petroleum 6 An oily, black substance that is found naturally underground and can be burned as a fuel or processed to make other fuels such as gasoline or kerosene. It is often called oil.

resale value 34 The value at which a person can sell a used item, especially a car.

rotary engine 44 A car engine in which a spinning three-sided piston replaces the up-and-down piston.

running boards 15 Flat rails located under the doors of cars of the 1920s and 1930s. They served as a step for passengers getting into and out of the cars.

supercharger 14, 15, 19, 21 An engine-driven pump that rams gas-air mixture into an engine, generating more power than the engine would normally produce.

turbocharger 38 A spinning, pumplike device that forces extra gas-air mixture into an engine, creating extra power. A turbocharger is spun by the force of hot exhaust gas rushing through it.

wind tunnel 40 A machine for testing how wind flows over a car body. A model of the car is placed inside the machine, and measurements are made as a fan blows wind over the body.